Temple of Changes

...

Between
Earth and Mystery

Copyright © 2020 by Elise Kost

All rights reserved. This book or any portion thereof may not be reproduced or used in any form or by any means whatsoever without the express written permission of the author, Elise Kost.

First Printing: 02.02.2020

ISBN 978-1-73432-130-2

elise kost
PO Box 737
Joshua Tree, CA 92252

www.templeofchanges.com

Temple of Changes
Between
Earth and Mystery

~<<< + >>>~

elise kost
2020

~

*Allow Freedom to Breathe You
by making Space within yourSelf
and All that Is*

~

~~~>>>+<<<~~~

For my mother, Gisa, whose respect for Nature, courage, creativity, and humble wisdom has inspired me and guided me all of my life. My greatest teacher and dearest friend :: I am eternally grateful for your honesty, kindness, and generous joy in helping things grow ~ your steady devotion and playful curiosity with all you create continues to show me The Way.

Gisa, age 19

~

*i am emptiness, listening (((
i am everything and no such thing
(a feather, a blade :: sometimes the same)
i am only following…
the breath…
one moment … to the next*

~

~<<<+>>>~

My gratitude for loved ones could fill a book in itself :: listing everyone who has touched and tuned my life is impossible.
You know who you are.
This life, this collection, even just one poem, wouldn't have been born without the vast support of Tribe, and the powerful spectrum of our light~shadow lives :: agonizing heart breaks; countless experiences of loss and confusion; moments of magnificent awe; magical, profound beauty.., and the breathlessness behind each enchantment.

THANK YOU for helping bring this whisper to form ::
Gisa; Diana Durr; Alberto + The Four Winds allyu;
Dean Taraborelli; Sir Willis; and Don, for calling this forth.

~ front cover art by Gisa
~ cover tech by Diana Durr
~ author photos by Elena Ray

~<<<+>>>~

~ <<< + >>> ~

Contents

...

I. letting go...1
    lay down...3
    circle of life...4
    fully empty..5
    how deep...6
    wind sings...7
    sage..8
    the pearl..9
    gone...10
    Free...11
    alive...12

II. curiosities and prayers..15
    wit..17
    hold me...18
    allow..19
    Stay...20
    the truth..21
    bend..22
    both...23
    jump...24
    change chases..25
    speak up..26
    circus..27

III. invitations...29
    blooming...31
    as is..32
    trust the whisper..33
    union...34
    steady..35
    if you must..36
    slow..37
    don't..38
    the edge..39
    children of the Phoenix...40
    be wisdom..41

IV. seasons, cycles, seeds 45
    hatch 47
    softer 48
    tendencies 49
    weightless 50
    freedom 51
    magnet 52
    growth 53
    pollen 54
    love all ways 55

V. Here 57
    choose 59
    reaching 60
    gentle 61
    claiming 62
    synthesis 63
    Annie 64
    whiskers 65
    essential sounds of light 66
    We 67
    settle 68

VI. Dragons 71
    glimpse 73
    the spiral 74
    canyon 75
    stillness 76
    delicate 77
    jade 78
    talons 79
    deeper 80
    One Wave 81

VII. soft sea breathing..85
       imagine...87
       following...88
       within..89
       silence...90
       love teaches..91
       just watch...92
       sing...93
       mountain..94
       the breeze..95
       beginnings...96

*I didn't trust it for a moment
but I drank it anyway -
the wine of my own poetry.
It gave me the daring
to take hold of the darkness
and to tear it into little pieces.*

~ 13th century, unknown

.I.

letting go

~

~ <<< + >>> ~

Lay down your sword,
in this Sacred circle.
and, Stand
...in Surrender.

Allow the Great River
to wash you : your purpose, and power.

your Path is now clear.

do not seek Grace,
Allow it to find you,
...by making Space,
within yourSelf
and All that Is.

pain yields
growth or strength
or something which will lead to a better place
in the end of it all,
or the middle,
or the beginning, again.

reluctantly
and with somewhat of a tucked tail,
I loosened my grip
on what I thought I knew.

I laid down my arrows of intention,
and aims of accomplishment.
I let my hair fall ~ down, down…down…to touch the Earth.
I let the Wind blow until my thoughts were strewn
    out of reach.
I let the Desert Summer Heat…
melt my need……
to control….

I sat and sat and sat,
and sweat away all holding hopes,
any last lingering layers of judgements ::
of self~other, trust~doubt, light~dark, love~pain
…same same same…..

I had to…
    dissolve…
        down, down, down …beyond the bones,
to release The Ancient Anger (mine and not mine).
to let go
of saying-doing-thinking
the "right" thing.

and at last, sink and surrender….
down, down, down….
into the depths of emptiness
where only No-thing and No-doing was left.

then, and only then
could I *See* anything.

Stay.

as the Wind
        whirls twists spins spits howls whips breaks betrays
Stay.

Stand Still.

Stand in the Center of the Wild unknown
Stand in the middle of your heartache and
Stop
trying to fix it.

Stay…there,
in the darkness of all that feels lost
…and rest.

Allow your pain to show you how deep
your Love goes
and then…, let go.
Let go of it all…
All the wanting - wishing - rearranging - aiming to change
to be better, be other, belong….

Allow the Wind to empty you
let the Truth, of this moment, breathe you.

Listen….

searching for the next hold
my fingertips caress the curves
of the cliffs I cling to
until the wind sings
and the pain of gripping is so strong
that the veins are ripping in my arms
and I know
I should just
let
go.

i relax into the shadows of The Sage

i listen

i pray

Show Me The Way.

On the 49th day
I climbed and crawled up the mountain
Rocks like blades under my feet
every edge reminding me
of every inability
on my knees, yet entirely free.

i buried prayers in the wild earth
the desert beyond my reach
the longing of my dreams…

i took one step at a time
breathing…being alive…just that.

the miracle of a moment
without wanting, just watching
without aiming
without trying to give enough
…just listening
…to the infinite quiet
inside Everything

i heard the Sun
pulsing on the the sand
i heard the Wind in my hands
i heard the Rivers of all lands
and the Earth, receiving my pause
as she carried me
through the vast calm sky
Moon of my Mind
Pearl, Divine.

Everywhere Beauty Breathes
silence to sound
all The Way around
beyond and between … *We Are Love.*

fresh ink under skin.

...whispers
     down alleys
          of a long time ago.

...layers peeling
    like pages of Prayers
            getting lost in the wind...

ever feel like you're just waiting
to kick your craving
without saving a single breath of strength
for the occasion?
...waiting for the fog to lift
standing on the curb to a cliff
leaning into the wind, clinging,
never knowing if courage might crumble?
stumbling along in the concrete jungle....

ever blame your briefcase hurry
'cuz tomorrow still looks blurry?
don't pass on your fury, man,
you gotta set yourself free!

ever feel like you got stripped of your ticket?
winding your path through the thinning thicket?
grinning your way into the racket-
missed the mark, couldn't stack it
slipped on your tact-
tripped your own trap?

... it's a big lap to swim
it's a long life to question
if you don't like guessing
but that's the lesson....
you just gotta set yourself free,
set yourself FREE.

how many millions of ways have been written about letting go?
songs of … 'let it be'?
how many voices, for how many lifetimes…
and Here We Are, still stunned by it.

we practice, again and again, practice
we expand, contract, rest and catch…
and still, there is more to learn.

Letting Go … is an infinite quest
there is only more - *emptiness*….
It travels much farther than any mind could go…

Trust, friend,
Be with it as it is, until it finds its way through

Trust in whatever you adore and cherish it
Allow it to nourish your devotion.

Letting go and being with,
Breathing this moment,
Is the purest Love Alive.

~ <<< + >>> ~

~ <<< + >>> ~

.II.

curiosities and prayers

~

~ <<< + >>> ~

The world stretches,
sensations bewitch,
every which way twitches.
I itch in my inabilities
in this world, inhibited
sitting lonely
with only
intentions
of wit.

Sacred ground
Hold me down, today
Hold me down.

my love is far away…
it's hard to stay, here, now.

Great Winds
bring me back my breath,
fill this hollow in my chest,
this infinite emptiness…
remind me : I am not alone.

Hold me down to the Earth
Hold me down.
let me feel my fire, tended
let my surrender, be safe
Hold me down.
let me receive your strength, today
Hold me down.
Softness and Grace : Guide The Way.

i bow
to enter
this small circle
of young cedars

i kneel
on the soft earth
and pray.

i release, let go, let be.

i smell their curiosity
as i reach to remember
how to move with such ease ~

some branches, heavy with berries
Seeds of ideas

…waiting…

for the appropriate moment to

Open
 and
Allow

the
next
step
.

Grasses quiver
as surrounding space breathes

what is it to be
rooted in stone and clay
and swept away
when the river runs

always reaching
for a deeper hold
and stretching high into the light
no matter what.

fearless, brave, bold.
wild mane of this Earth
resilient, flexible,
abundant, humble, and Strong.

Show Me The Way
of softness and surrender

Show Me The Way
of motivation and grace

Show Me courage and commitment

Show Me how to Stay
when Silence sings her song.

The truth is
sometimes we have to scream for help to get it.

- now I got it
clear as a crystal
by the way we're blowin our whistles
that we'd rather only feel-hear-see-taste-touch-smell
the ripe ripe fruit of life
and leave the birth-growth-death-and decay in the closet
tied up and out of luck
to be a good lesson learned.

And the truth is, I feel the Earth creaking,
like the last board on the bridge about to break.

And the truth is,
We need to start listening to our bodies again…
(kneel into the sand, let yourself sigh)
~ like the sound of wind whispering trees,
and Hawk, as she flies ~

And the truth is…
I see beauty and I want it inside me,
(how was I born so distracted and always so hungry?)
…I wonder why everything has to rhyme somewhere,
like it's all a puzzle and I have to find the way
it all fits together -
like the way some people live on time -
by time, bound by time, surrounded by time -
I'm a slave to the rhyme
to the rhythm in my blood, my soul ~
Always yearning….for the WHOLE.

blood on my fingertips

i think it's from clinging to rock
with an overwhelming desperation
to defeat something inside me
that doesn't listen.

i want to bend backwards,
neck thrust,
and still be understood.

entangled in the human condition
i am swaying on the swing
of the vast paradox
between passion and pause
...i am Both
velvet and claws.

i jumped into the water face first with a grin,
found myself swimming in you,
then sinking.

i came up for breath
from what i was drinking
beneath your surface.

i saw my reflection.
i saw everything.
before
i felt myself slipping
hitting the shore with a slap,
kicking, but not turning back.

don't title me
no labels
no advertisements here.

truth chases everything
that changes this body,
this bible of mind
which is mine
to leave
untitled.

I have no idea what you're saying,
your language twisted by someone else's rope.

I'm looking for inspiration in still life
and you're on the phone counting in Latin.

I'm climbing the staircase of solitude to freedom,
you're irony in a circle chair, squared.

I'm either smoke from your chimney
or the reflection below-
I'm hungry
I'm silent
I'm broken and slow.

I'm bright and blue, brown, green, and grey,
I'm crazy and sexy
your scorpion and your prey.

I'm your simple, your psychic,
your heroine, your plea.

…I have no idea
what you're saying
to me.

there's a reward
for your strife,
if you pay attention,
to your purpose
in this circus
life

~ <<< + >>> ~

.III.

invitations

~

~ <<< + >>> ~

We Are the guardians and guides of
unmanifest Creation energy
of the Divine Infinite Mystery
the quantum spectrum of possibility
the eternal wave, in motion

...even Stillness moves...
and stones will roll
the same Way water flows ~ ~ ~
with a little nudge...

The Way always points to The Path
may we relax
breathe
walk free
and
be in service
to Beauty
..listening..
to the Holy Medicine
of this Moment.

We Are Everything.

YES
is a flower blooming
from our darkness.

Incessantly striving to improve,
to be approved of,
to prove one's worth,
is exhausting.

What is of more value
than the lack of this -
than TRUST in AS IS?

Fire burns.
Salt pulls.
Oil soothes.
Water, moves.

The eternity
inside every moment
holds
the most devoted lover of all time ::
   the enveloping embrace,
       of suspending the mind.

Have Courage
to be open,
to trust
the Wisdom of the Whisper
the subtle ripple
the clear and simple

Listen...

what binds you?
what needs renewing?
what wants to sing through you?
...for the Love of All.

Judging the problem,
even your own doubt,
or why-when-where-with whom you close your Heart...
is not useful
for your Joy, wholeness, or sense of belonging.
Nor is it useful for the problem itself,
or any darkness anywhere.

Breathe softly,
rest in The Unknown we ALL walk.

Step gently,
Like the Leopard
   Be Fierce Grace
   with your Truth.
   ...whiskers spanning both shadow and light.

The world needs your Wisdom.
Speak bravely.
Share generously, the gift of your wild and sweet LOVE.

The space between us is smaller than you know.
In fact, there is no such thing.

Trees root and Stars shine.

What exists beyond the fragrance of fascination
reveals itself only in
Union.

surrender.
release, relax, retrieve your self.
relieve your self of satisfaction.
surrender.
steady your mirror.

Swim through the shadow of your greatest fear.

Water! Fire! Wind! Earth!

s p a c e

light, shadow
animal, man

Trust.

movement
stillness

Beauty.

…breath…

if you must seek,
seek Harmony
among these things.

We All Belong
in this life of loss and blossom.

Death..is energy moving ~
shape shifting form
The Wave, always changing
there is only Light, pulsing…
Wind…
Sun on skin…
…there is but One Infinite Breath
and We are it, baby.

Relax, rest
inside who you are.

Pain makes space.
Allow the Heart ache to open you
into a wider sky.

Love takes care of itself.
…let it be, let it go.

Breathe…
deep..soft..slow ~

eleven months of solitude
after a lifetime of serving what's been asked of you
eleven months passed…

eighty-four thousand aspects of delusion, desire, hate
are a lot to face, despite regret
and then even more when they become less.

take your best guess
but don't just stab in the dark—
something may be dodging
don't just sit there in park
(don't deny the heart)
don't stand in the yard
and stare at every choice flying past you
every result refracting
slowly retracting any sense of satisfaction.

eleven months, of silent action.

The Ocean of infinite possibility
swims inside invisibility ::
amidst majestic mountains
                beyond mountains
                              of mystical beauty ~

To find the jewel of your quest
Lay down your fear,
and climb with your best.

The Edge
is
Here.

The immortality of Love
rests
in the valley of Stillness
where the mist
whispers ::

You are all ways returning, until you arrive.
All you need do is breathe, to be inspired.

let the Great Fire ignite you
All the Way, All the Way

feel the Fire rise high – clear the mind
pull it with your breath, feed it – feed it!
let it clean your confusion,
weave it through every space in you that needs it!
Deep through the marrow of this precious life.

You Are the Light of the Mystery!

Mastery is Allowing ::
~ the Wheel of Wisdom
~ the Realizing Witness
~ Listening to the Stillness
~ singing, dancing, praising ::
all the beauty, *all* the pain

let the Great Fire ignite you
All the Way, All the Way ~ !!

it's easy to trust and coast in the flow of tenderness
but when the road gets rough,
we Must listen
and pause
if we are lost.

we sing :
Holy Holy let it rain down Wisdom
All is welcome Here.

We are Divine drops of Star Light
breathing through blood and bone and heat
finding Truth
through tension and release.

May we remember
We are the Gold
of those who came before us
and we nourish those to come
by Allowing Love in ~

through our Hearts and hands,
may we give generously
may we gather gratitude so there is plenty plenty
may we receive All the Beauty we believe in
and beyond ~ ~ ~
and may we Breathe
JOY
through every root-vein-branch-bloom-fruit-AND seed!

May we BE the Wisdom we wish to see!

~ <<< + >>> ~

*One instant is eternity,
eternity is now.
When you see through this one instant,
you see through the one who sees.*

~ Wu-Men

~ <<< + >>> ~

.IV.

seasons, cycles, seeds

~

~ <<< + >>> ~

i'm not gonna ask
i'm not gonna ask
i'm not gonna ask
you
with butterfly wings for legs
open open open yourself
so you can see
beyond body

dance to be free!

bite bite bite bite bite
until you break the skin of self
and hatch
until you don't need
to ask.

...after three million,
two hundred seventy-four thousand,
six hundred,
and
nineteen years...
of navigating the Underground River of Sorrow ~ ~ ~

i found myself.

...in a field
of faery blue butterflies
dancing around my ankles,
as i rediscovered how to walk
with Softness and Surrender.

...i found myself
in a grove
of Laughing aspen
and dandelion leaves begging to be harvested -
medicine for the bleeding woman i am.

i found myself
among blooming wild berries,
not in a hurry to be ripe or ready,
and mullein leaves -
softer than my first kiss,
reminding me of my Life, *Alive*.

like the paper cup
sipped by lips after lips
leaks

like the prophet's pocket
picked
for a bigger place
on the porch of grace

old divinity
folded over and over
tends to crease

weightless

    the body lifts,

Earth, in perspective
brings the Ocean of emptiness
to surface

what is, is.

nothing can be done
with rejection
other than to breathe…to receive it,
and know ::

Wholeness
reveals itself
through cracks, crevices, folds,
valleys, mountains, and rivers…

whether you're afraid or bold,
Love will find you.

Freedom is
lightening along the spine
~ serpentine river of light.

Freedom is
facing the fire
feeling the heat
and, letting it be.

Freedom is
dancing the flames
riding the waves
~ compassion, resilience, grace ~
finding, the Middle Way.

the nature of mind
is a pool of time
reflecting various ways to survive

every small death
ripples into the memory
and middle of me

magnets to beauty, to love, to truth,
simply put, there is no proof
that We Are nothing
but that which moves

One illusion to the next,
life is what we make of it.

last night i looked deep into the widow's eyes...
vulnerable, soft, kind...
shining black yet full of light

i could have stayed and wept with her,
asked her questions
and complimented her beauty

but..., she was a black widow,
only a fool would lean in closer
to hear the whisper
behind her allure

when i awoke,
the Phoenix laughed

Courage does not grow through only kissing butterflies.

There are 10,000 things to do
plus one.
They will never be done.

And anyway,
how can one do anything,
when there is LOVE to be made?

...

We melt into the moment
in between the notes
the sigh inside the song -
isn't there always one?
Isn't there always a pause
a blossom...pollen...a loss?

Oh love, oh breath,
please let us rest
in the Space Between,
in the always beckoning Balance,
in the ever open Beauty ~

Radiant Emptiness
just do, just be.

Sacred Holy Magnetic Moment
Opens

i breathe ...

The Great River of movement
Receives
quiet imagination and belief.

i dare not ask my reflection,
washed away,
about the truth of time...

i only know this -
Love always changes
and
Love, always Is.

~ <<< + >>> ~

.V.

Here

~

~ <<< + >>> ~

when time stands still, We Listen

the infinite Quest of Love
always beckoning, beginning,
Here and beyond ~ ~ ~

We Listen
(birds sing)
Beloved, carry on
the Way is clear
the Way is *through*

Yes. We see you.

Trust.
and please
go softly, go slowly
go easy....

Courage :: carry us
through this Medicine of Mystery
for We Are
growing into
wise trees,
roots deep -
and yes,
we have grieved
and yes,
we celebrate our strong bodies - bridges to the light
and yes,
we reach high where the beauty is so bright -
the bloom, so enchanting
we have yet to taste the fruits.

the Truth is
We Are All Seasons
in any moment

One Breath
at a time,
We *Choose*.

reaching to repeat
the gifts of the Mystery
this sweet moment
reminds me,
it is lost
when we seek.

dancing aspen
gentle joy
whispering grace
into sharp edges
of tricky terrain

every trail has its teacher,
its perfect fit.
see it or not - fix it or flop it,
We All fall…

and Rise!
transparent wings of butterflies!
sighs of relief
just to Be
Alive.

I protect
The Quest.
Divine Mystical Stillness, Movement, and Light!
I protect prayer
the longing
the lost
inspiration
Beauty
LOVE
Freedom
and…the soft.
I protect
The Sword.
the whisper…
the flutter
the hint, the Wind
the flow ~
the Unknown…
I protect Growth.
Sincerity.
I protect the Power of Alchemy.
Body.
Mountains, Valleys, and the Space in Between)))
I protect The Embrace
The Moon, the Sun, Truth
The Journey
of Pain, and Grace.

know thySelf
listen to Wholeness
Trust the Mysterious
Open
into the Heart of
Synthesis

the waves of The Ocean
are never the same.

practicing,
polishing,
nourishing the genuine

catching the pearl
to let it go
give it away
watch it grow
again and again,
beginning, listening

when in doubt,
pause,
then *carry on*.

Hands like clouds...
                              far out...

Don't Try Anything.

death is only the breath shifting shape
We Are the Owl, the Bobcat, the Breeze...
One infinite moment of Love,
aware, awake.

i live among cacti, howls, and claws
where scorpions sting and the tortoise crawls…

my strong body
like a boulder
not easy to budge
but good for leaning on
to rest and remember…

my whiskers, listen…

to the magnetic electric always begging to become
luring to the next layer
of…Trust

essence, nature, power, grace
luminous emptiness
to be filled and expressed

breathe your mind open
the way the sky fire opens the flower

balance
on the edge of the sword,
between the dual blades
like surfing the waves
of the human heart

beware the enchantment of form, of sensation
flow and friction are always teaching

inside - outside
alignment
refining
finding the essential
again and again

let Truth soothe you
You Are Here
and always have been.

The women of my tribe are a Wild garden,
growing.
My women move me,
with their honesty, humility, courage, grace, loyalty.
They are brave and loving, forgiving, patient, and WISE.
They have ...::: no age :::... and ~ clear eyes ~

My women dance barefoot, wear boots and action shoes -
they eat when hungry,
sway their hips with the moon,
and bow... to what's True.

My women share and trust, empower and adore.
My women love fiercely and softly, sweetly and sincerely.
My sisters are honey, and pepper -
scented of Earth and *All Weathers*.
My sisters aren't afraid to shake their tail feathers~
or fly ~ ~ ~
when it's time
to Rise.

These women - have nothing to hide!
These women, We Are vast open skies ~
We make Love with the Sun,
our wombs are the Ocean.

Come,
come climb the mountains of our minds
and see with us,
the *light* beyond time ~ ~ ~

We Are Water Wind Fire Earth and Mystery, in Sacred skin.
We Are Galaxies of glory and dust.
We Are beauty and pain, bold and brave,
We Are change.

Crystals of light, We Are
Anchored in life, We Are

We Are impossible miracles
...molecular microbes...
We Are moving fractals of stars
Waves and particles...
made of yesterdays and tomorrows
arriving one moment at a time ~
All sensing, and,,, blind....

We Are attachment, and letting go
We Are habit : a mess...yes, we are wrecked -
yet
We Are the breath inside Breath,
We Are Great Awareness
We Are evolution - The Dance
We Are the blood of Earth, finding balance (again and again)....

We Are feline, raptor, serpent, and snail
We Are desire.
We Are prayer.
We Are Stillness and space beyond space)))
We Are ancient
and,, nothing but babies....

We Are Truth.
We Are Grace.

We Are trees, the way of the bee, and
We Are the honey, the heat
and the song of a
single blossom.

We rise and reach deep,
We Are seasons, cycles, seeds
always rolling and always Here ....

We Are the flaming light of life ~
We Are everything, everything at the same time!

there is no reason or way to explain
the journey we all take
day by day..staying awake, for Love.

exhale and let go,,, settle thy Fire
Soften,,, rest on the Earth that gave you form

you are safe Here :: allow the Winds to Breathe you
move like Water ~ ~ ~
   follow the waves of Ease ~ through completion.

...when in doubt, Open and Listen......
find the whisper that precedes every belief

. do not try to be more or less .

for the benefit of All :: be who and where You Are
((there is nothing better))
this nourishes the Ultimate :: Love.

~ <<< + >>> ~

God breaks the heart again and again and again, until it stays open.

~ Hazrat Inayat Khan

.VI.

Dragons

~

~ <<< + >>> ~

the Wind
of the Dragon's wings
winds itself through my whiskers
of Awareness

slowly…

like Water between roots
of bamboo

always just enough

…like a glimpse
of You.

…like mist which moves
        among mountains
              … slowly… slowly …

what is the distance between Rain and the River?

what is this space   between   you and me?

…what to keep…what to release…
…the balance of create and receive

every new now,
        breathing …

                      bamboo sways
                      always changing
                      subtle,
                      certain.

                      i pray
                      and still,
                      i yearn.

~

i will meet You
in Reverence
of calm and quiet
of soft and stable and steady
of the swift, slow..., and strong
of Space
of the Way through ~
Here,,, and Beyond

~

this desert canyon lives ten thousand miles deep
it twists and turns
as it yearns
for rain to run its river
to be filled to the rim
to reach the sea
to sing the song, of belonging
to touch somewhere new,
in me.

One pink blossom
Aside thorns, no one.

Morning dew soothes.
Soft moss.
Sight, sighs.

The Sword
stands,
shimmers,
then falls away....

Only *We* remain

inside *One* gown
of the *Sea*
in between .. moments,,
~ moving...

...Lavender Skies...
Moon,, Rises

New webs cross the path
among blackberry vines and tall grass.

Birds Sing.
delicate timing.
Eyes bring
soft surrendering.

moon.
midnight.
roots reach for stars.
leaves release rain.
crimson sings.

Sun Rises
Jade Flower Opens
Water Wisdom Illuminates
the ever moving ~ Union

soft, genuine
Mystery whispering

Dragon, talons
release me.

let me rest.

Here.
in between…
in the vast,
expanding
Beauty,
breathing…

Herons are dragons, don't you know?
So when I watched them part ways above the trees
It was like worlds ending
Opening into a new sky

Holding space for love is not enough.

Going deeper means
Covering the wood pile before it rains
And
Allowing more in than the heart can hold.

Slowly, slowly, we all soften.

transparent silver dew, sits.

i wait

for The Way
through…

to reveal itself
from within
from the depths of all i've been
and held onto
…i let go.

i feel my bones
breathing
i feel empty of 'me'
filled with essence of ease
clarity, without knowing
bamboo, just growing

soft earth…weight sinks
soft silk…mist lifts

whiskers listen
precision whispering wisdom
gentle and genuine
translucent, luminous, infinite openness

exquisite profound Mystery

roots reach, branches sway
leaves fall…
One Wave.

~ <<< + >>> ~

*old pond
frog jumps in
splash.*

~ Basho

.VII.

soft sea breathing

~

~ <<< + >>> ~

I am the rainbow, the mountain, the stones, the earth,
I am the wind, the water, the sun, rebirth
I am the dream, the sorrow, the shadow and light
I am *everything* we have ALL been -
the memory dancing ~

I am humbled every day
by the beauty and the pain ::

We all have pain of one kind or another
just like we all have love for something -

and I am in love with the Mystery beyond me,
the sensations through me,
the poetry ~
I am in love with LOVE
and the vision of what could be ~
…how small we are, *and* how POWERFUL we can be!

We Are Free!

what we see and sculpt
of each day
each moment
each creation,
can only be as good
as the pulp
of our own imagination.

Rising
and
deepening
into and through
the Vast Sacred of All
questions dissolve

the vessel opens, fills, empties, breathes,
listens, surrenders, allows Love,
in ease ~

at last, relaxed
following softness
following space
~ the Mystery in these
again and again, enchanting me ~

find Stillness within
Trust in the cycles of Life
we are all learning

i cannot speak louder than silence.
though i try and try
i am distracted by what i cannot say.

Yes grief,
but harmony still.

Breathe your relief,
Love reaches for us each.

dragonfly sits on rock
water falls
just watch

Love sings us forward
Breath sings us through
Joy sings us into the infinite

Beauty, is always true.

Still Mountain
Standing

True Heart
Resting

Resounding Softness

looking through circles
across sand and sun
i sit
thinking about being more organized
with my collections of minds,
but the distraction of the trees
quivering in the breeze
leaves me figuring that time is just a tease
and i, am at peace, again.

i watched the Sky bleed open
deep red burning into a new Beginning
bright mandarin
melting into ancient familiar gold
crown of the Earth
radiating under a soft, washed
infinite lilac and rose…
Mountains like indigo elephants
sleeping in the shadows
waiting to be kissed into life by light
revealing every wrinkle, story
touching even the potential of…*More*
    more mystery
        more beauty
            more wild stillness
to awaken into an
ever expanding Ocean ~
            …of *Peace*.

~ <<< + >>> ~

*The fish trap exists because of the fish;
once you've gotten the fish, you can forget the trap.*

*The rabbit snare exists because of the rabbit;
once you've gotten the rabbit, you can forget the snare.*

*Words exist because of meaning;
once you've gotten the meaning, you can forget the words.*

*Where can I find a man who has forgotten the words
so I can have a word with him?*

~ Chuang Tzu

about the author

~

Over the last two decades, Elise has guided individuals and groups to claim courage and more fully personify their beauty and joyful vitality of body, heart-mind, and spirit. In addition to celebrating life through poetry and creating custom adornments to enhance and enchant through form, Elise is a master certified energy medicine practitioner, ceremonialist, mentor, and spiritual teacher. Greatly influenced by Nature and devoted to the Mystery, Elise helps others (re)discover the Sacred ~ deepen their sense of trust, passion, empowerment, and LOVE for the transformational journey of creating a conscious, embodied way of wisdom, peace and inspiration.

Elise lives in the Mojave Desert of Joshua Tree, California.

To purchase a spoken word version of these poems,
or to connect with Elise, find her through her website :
www.TempleOfChanges.com

~ <<< + >>> ~

Be brave. Be yourSelf.
Love the choices you make or make different ones.
Trust yourSelf.

the Harmony of
~ Empowered Embodiment ~
and
~ Humble Receptivity ~
begins
Within

www.ingramcontent.com/pod-product-compliance
Lightning Source LLC
Chambersburg PA
CBHW031156160426
43193CB00008B/391